The Ultimate Prioritization Guide

Achieve More with Less Stress

HARRELL HOWARD

Table of Contents

Introduction 6
    The Modern Dilemma: Overwhelm and Stress 6
    What is Prioritization? 7
    Why This Book? 8

Chapter 1: Understanding the Importance of Prioritization 11
    The Science Behind Prioritization 11
        Cognitive Load Theory 11
        How the Brain Processes Tasks and Decisions 12
    Consequences of Poor Prioritization 13
        Burnout and Stress 13
        Missed Opportunities and Inefficiencies 14
    Benefits of Effective Prioritization 15
        Increased Productivity and Efficiency 15
        Better Work-Life Balance and Reduced Stress 16

Chapter 2: Common Prioritization Pitfalls and How to Avoid Them 18
    The Myth of Multitasking 18
        Why Multitasking Doesn't Work 19
        The Impact of Switching Costs on Productivity 20
        How to Avoid the Multitasking Trap 20
    Procrastination and Perfectionism 21
        The Role of Fear and Self-Doubt in Poor Prioritization 21
        Strategies to Overcome These Obstacles 22
    The Urgency Trap 23
        Differentiating Between Urgent and Important Tasks 24
        How to Avoid Getting Caught in the Urgency Trap 25

Chapter 3: Proven Prioritization Frameworks 27
    The Eisenhower Matrix 27
        Quadrants of Urgency and Importance 27

Practical Examples and Applications	28
The ABCDE Method	30
Categorizing Tasks by Importance	30
How to Apply This Method in Daily Planning	30
The 80/20 Rule (Pareto Principle)	31
Focusing on the Vital Few Tasks That Yield the Most Results	31
Case Studies of the 80/20 Rule in Action	32
MoSCoW Method	33
Use Cases for Project Management and Personal Tasks	33
Chapter 4: Personalizing Your Prioritization Strategy	**36**
Assessing Your Current Prioritization Habits	36
Exercises for Self-Reflection	36
Identifying Strengths and Weaknesses	38
Aligning Prioritization with Goals	39
Setting SMART Goals	39
How to Ensure Your Prioritization Supports Your Long-Term Objectives	40
Building a Flexible Prioritization System	41
Adapting to Changing Circumstances	41
Creating a System That Evolves with Your Needs	42
Chapter 5: Prioritization in the Workplace	**45**
Prioritizing in a Team Environment	45
Balancing individual and team priorities	45
Communicating priorities effectively with colleagues	46
Managing Competing Priorities	47
Strategies for negotiation and compromise	48
Handling conflicting demands from managers and stakeholders	49
Tools and Techniques for Workplace Prioritization	50
Using project management tools	50
Time-blocking and calendar management	51
Chapter 6: Prioritization Techniques for Personal Life	**53**
Balancing Work and Personal Life	53

    The importance of setting boundaries — 53
    Strategies for time management outside of work — 54
  Prioritizing Health and Well-being — 55
    How to make self-care a priority — 55
    The link between well-being and productivity — 56
  Managing Household and Family Priorities — 57
    Techniques for shared prioritization with family members — 57
    Prioritization in parenting and home management — 58

Chapter 7: Prioritization in the Digital Age — 60
  Managing Digital Overload — 60
    Strategies for minimizing digital distractions — 60
    Tools for managing emails, notifications, and social media — 61
  Prioritization with Digital Tools — 62
    Apps and software that assist with prioritization — 62
    Pros and cons of digital versus analog prioritization methods — 63
  The Role of Automation in Prioritization — 63
    How to use automation to reduce workload and focus on important tasks — 63
    Examples of automation tools and their uses — 64

Chapter 8: Developing Long-Term Prioritization Habits — 66
  Creating Sustainable Habits — 66
    The importance of consistency and discipline — 66
    Techniques for building and maintaining prioritization habits — 67
  Periodic Review and Adjustment — 68
    The role of regular reviews in effective prioritization — 68
    How to adjust your priorities as life circumstances change — 69
  Overcoming Setbacks and Staying on Track — 70
    Strategies for dealing with disruptions and setbacks — 70
    How to regain focus after a lapse in prioritization — 71

My Final Word: The Path to a Balanced and Productive Life — 73
  Recap of Key Principles — 73
  The Ongoing Journey of Prioritization — 74

    Understanding that prioritization is a continuous process   74
    Encouragement to keep refining and adapting prioritization strategies   75
  Final Words of Encouragement   76

Appendices   79

  Appendix A: Prioritization Worksheets   79
  Appendix B: Recommended Reading and Resources   80
    Books   80
    Tools   80
  Appendix C: Glossary of Terms   81

Introduction

Let's imagine you're sitting at your desk, staring at an endless to-do list. Your phone's buzzing with notifications, your inbox is overflowing, and you've got a stack of papers demanding your attention. Sound familiar? Welcome to the modern world, where being busy is a badge of honor, and stress is the unwelcome companion we've all grown accustomed to.

But what if I told you there's a better way? A way to take control of your time, your tasks, and your life? That's exactly what this book is about. We're going to dive deep into the art and science of prioritization – the secret weapon of the most successful and balanced individuals in today's fast-paced world.

The Modern Dilemma: Overwhelm and Stress

Let's face it: we're living in an age of information overload. Technology has connected us in ways we never thought possible, but it's also created a never-ending stream of demands on our attention. Your smartphone alone is a portal to a world of endless possibilities – and endless distractions.

Remember when you could leave work at the office? Now, work follows us everywhere. That ping from your boss at 9 PM? It's hard to ignore. That brilliant idea that pops into your head at 2 AM? You feel compelled to jot it down before it vanishes.

And it's not just work. Our personal lives are busier than ever. Social media keeps us constantly connected (and constantly comparing ourselves to others). Online shopping means we can buy anything, anytime. Streaming services offer us more entertainment than we could consume in a lifetime.

All these choices might seem like a good thing. After all, isn't having options better than not having them? But here's the kicker: too many choices can be paralyzing. Psychologists call it "decision fatigue" – the more choices we have to make, the worse we become at making them. By the end of the day, we're so mentally exhausted that choosing what to have for dinner feels like solving a complex math equation.

What is Prioritization?

So, what's the solution to this modern madness? Enter prioritization – your new superpower in the battle against overwhelm and stress.

At its core, prioritization is the art of deciding what's truly important and focusing your time and energy on those things. It's about making conscious choices about where to invest your most precious resources – your time and attention.

But prioritization isn't just about getting more done. It's about getting the right things done. It's the difference between being busy and being productive. Between running on a hamster wheel and actually moving forward in life.

When you master prioritization, you'll find that you can:

- Accomplish more in less time
- Reduce stress and anxiety
- Improve the quality of your work
- Create more time for the things you love
- Feel more in control of your life

Sounds pretty good, right?

Why This Book?

Now, you might be thinking, "Prioritization sounds great, but how do I actually do it?" That's exactly why I wrote this book.

In the pages that follow, we're going to explore practical, proven strategies for prioritization. We'll look at why our brains struggle with prioritization and how to overcome these natural tendencies. We'll dive into different prioritization frameworks and learn how to apply them in both our personal and professional lives.

But this isn't just another dry, theoretical book. I'm going to share real-life examples, personal anecdotes, and practical exercises that you can start using today. By the time you finish this book, you'll have a personalized prioritization system that works for you.

Here's what you can expect to learn:

- The science behind prioritization and why it's so crucial in today's world
- Common prioritization pitfalls and how to avoid them
- Proven prioritization frameworks used by successful individuals and organizations
- How to create a personalized prioritization strategy that aligns with your goals
- Techniques for prioritizing in the workplace, even when dealing with competing demands

- Strategies for prioritizing your personal life and maintaining work-life balance
- How to use technology to enhance your prioritization efforts (without letting it become a distraction)
- Tips for developing long-term prioritization habits that stick

Whether you're a busy professional trying to climb the corporate ladder, an entrepreneur juggling multiple projects, a student balancing studies and social life, or simply someone who wants to get more out of each day, this book is for you.

So, are you ready to take control of your time, reduce your stress, and start achieving more of what truly matters to you? Let's dive in and unlock the power of prioritization.

Chapter 1: Understanding the Importance of Prioritization

Have you ever had one of those days where you're busy from dawn to dusk, but at the end of it, you feel like you've accomplished nothing? You're not alone. Many of us confuse being busy with being productive. But here's the truth: busyness without prioritization is like a hamster wheel – lots of effort, but no real progress.

Let's start by understanding why prioritization is so crucial in today's world, and how it can transform not just your productivity, but your entire approach to work and life.

The Science Behind Prioritization

To truly grasp the importance of prioritization, we need to take a quick dive into the fascinating world of cognitive science. Don't worry – I promise to keep it light and relevant!

Cognitive Load Theory

Have you ever tried to juggle while riding a unicycle? Probably not, because you intuitively understand that your brain can only handle so much at once. This is the basic idea behind Cognitive Load Theory.

Developed by Australian educational psychologist John Sweller in the 1980s, Cognitive Load Theory suggests that our working memory – the mental workspace where we process information – has a limited capacity. When we exceed this capacity, our ability to think clearly and make decisions diminishes.

Think about it like this: your working memory is like a small table. You can only fit so many items on it before things start falling off the edges. When you prioritize, you're essentially deciding which items deserve a spot on that table, and which can wait their turn.

How the Brain Processes Tasks and Decisions

Every time you're faced with a task or decision, your brain goes through a complex process:

1. It assesses the importance and urgency of the task.
2. It considers the potential outcomes and consequences.
3. It evaluates the resources (time, energy, skills) required to complete the task.

4. It compares this task with other pending tasks.

This process happens so quickly that we're often not even aware of it. But here's the catch: the more tasks and decisions we face, the more our brain has to work. And just like a muscle, our brain can get tired.

This is where prioritization comes in. By consciously deciding what's important ahead of time, we reduce the number of decisions our brain needs to make on the fly. It's like creating a pre-approved guest list for that table in your working memory.

Consequences of Poor Prioritization

Now that we understand how our brain deals with tasks and decisions, let's look at what happens when we don't prioritize effectively.

Burnout and Stress

I remember a time early in my career when I thought saying "yes" to every project and task was the key to success. I was working 14-hour days, juggling multiple projects, and constantly feeling like I was dropping balls.

The result? I burned out. Hard. I was stressed, irritable, and my work quality suffered. I learned the hard way that trying to do everything is a surefire path to accomplishing nothing – at least nothing well.

Burnout isn't just about feeling tired. It's a state of physical, emotional, and mental exhaustion that can lead to:

- Decreased productivity
- Increased errors in work
- Health problems (both physical and mental)
- Strained relationships
- Loss of motivation and creativity

By not prioritizing, we open ourselves up to these risks. We spread ourselves too thin, and everything suffers as a result.

Missed Opportunities and Inefficiencies

Poor prioritization doesn't just lead to burnout – it can also mean missing out on important opportunities.

When we fail to prioritize, we often end up spending too much time on low-value tasks. We get caught up in the minutiae, the busy work that feels productive but doesn't move the needle.

Meanwhile, the truly important tasks – the ones that could lead to a promotion, launch a successful business, or improve our personal relationships – get pushed to the back burner.

I once worked with a talented software developer who was always the last to leave the office. He prided himself on his work ethic, but he was so bogged down in answering every email and attending every meeting that he never had time for the innovative coding that could have advanced his career. By not prioritizing, he was efficient at the small things but ineffective at the big things.

Benefits of Effective Prioritization

Now that we've looked at the dark side of poor prioritization, let's shine a light on the benefits of doing it well.

Increased Productivity and Efficiency

When you prioritize effectively, you focus your energy on the tasks that matter most. This leads to:

- Higher quality work on important projects
- Faster completion of critical tasks
- Improved decision-making (because you're not mentally exhausted)
- Greater sense of accomplishment at the end of each day

I've seen this play out countless times in my own life. When I started rigorously prioritizing my tasks, I found that I could accomplish in 6 focused hours what used to take me 10 scattered hours.

Better Work-Life Balance and Reduced Stress

Perhaps the most significant benefit of effective prioritization is its impact on your overall quality of life.

When you prioritize well, you:

- Create clear boundaries between work and personal time
- Reduce the feeling of being overwhelmed
- Have more time for activities you enjoy
- Experience less guilt about unfinished tasks (because you know you're focusing on what's truly important)

- Sleep better (because your mind isn't racing with all the things you "should" be doing)

Prioritization isn't just about getting more done – it's about creating a life that feels balanced and fulfilling.

As we move forward in this book, we'll explore specific strategies and techniques for prioritization. But remember: at its core, prioritization is about aligning your actions with your values and goals. It's about making conscious choices about how you spend your time and energy.

In the next chapter, we'll look at some common prioritization pitfalls and how to avoid them. But before we do, take a moment to reflect on your current approach to prioritization. Are you often feeling overwhelmed? Do you struggle to focus on what's truly important? Recognizing where you are now is the first step towards mastering the art of prioritization.

Chapter 2: Common Prioritization Pitfalls and How to Avoid Them

We've all been there. You start the day with the best intentions, armed with a to-do list and a determination to be productive. But somehow, by the end of the day, you find yourself wondering where all the time went. If this sounds familiar, you're likely falling into some common prioritization traps.

In this chapter, we'll explore three of the biggest pitfalls that derail our prioritization efforts: the myth of multitasking, the twin demons of procrastination and perfectionism, and the urgency trap. More importantly, we'll discuss how to overcome these obstacles and set yourself up for prioritization success.

The Myth of Multitasking

In our fast-paced world, multitasking is often seen as a badge of honor. We pride ourselves on our ability to juggle multiple tasks at once. I used to brag about how I could participate in a conference call, respond to emails, and work on a presentation all at the same time. Spoiler alert: I wasn't doing any of those things well.

Why Multitasking Doesn't Work

Here's the hard truth: multitasking is a myth. What we think of as multitasking is actually task-switching, and it's terrible for our productivity. Here's why:

1. **Our brains aren't wired for it**: The human brain is designed to focus on one thing at a time. When we try to do multiple cognitive tasks simultaneously, we're actually forcing our brains to switch rapidly between tasks.
2. **It reduces efficiency**: Each time we switch tasks, there's a cognitive cost. Our brains need time to disengage from one task, switch to another, and then refocus. This switching time may only be a fraction of a second, but it adds up over the course of a day.
3. **It increases errors**: When we're constantly switching between tasks, we're more likely to make mistakes. We're not giving any one task our full attention, which means we're not doing our best work on any of them.
4. **It's stressful**: Constant task-switching can lead to mental fatigue and increased stress levels. It's like trying to watch three movies simultaneously

by constantly changing channels – exhausting and unsatisfying.

The Impact of Switching Costs on Productivity

Let's put some numbers to this. Studies have shown that it can take up to 23 minutes to fully refocus after switching tasks. If you switch tasks just 5 times in a day, that's nearly 2 hours of lost productivity!

I experienced this firsthand when I started tracking my time closely. I was shocked to discover how much time I was losing to task-switching. Once I started batching similar tasks together and focusing on one thing at a time, my productivity skyrocketed.

How to Avoid the Multitasking Trap

1. **Practice single-tasking**: Focus on one task at a time. Give it your full attention before moving on to the next.
2. **Use time-blocking**: Allocate specific blocks of time for different types of tasks. For example, set aside an hour for responding to emails rather than checking them constantly throughout the day.
3. **Minimize distractions**: Turn off notifications on your phone and computer when you need to

focus. Consider using apps that block distracting websites during work hours.
4. **Take regular breaks**: Our brains aren't designed for non-stop focus. Use techniques like the Pomodoro method (25 minutes of focused work followed by a 5-minute break) to maintain concentration.

Remember, the goal isn't to do more things at once, but to do the right things with full focus.

Procrastination and Perfectionism

Procrastination and perfectionism might seem like opposite problems, but they often go hand in hand. Both can be major obstacles to effective prioritization.

The Role of Fear and Self-Doubt in Poor Prioritization

At their core, both procrastination and perfectionism are often driven by fear and self-doubt.

Procrastination is usually about avoiding discomfort. We put off tasks because:

- We're afraid of failing

- The task seems overwhelming
- We're not sure where to start
- We doubt our ability to do it well

Perfectionism, on the other hand, is about setting unrealistically high standards. Perfectionists often:

- Spend too much time on unimportant details
- Struggle to complete tasks because they're never "good enough"
- Avoid starting tasks for fear of not doing them perfectly

Both of these tendencies can severely hamper our ability to prioritize effectively. We either avoid important tasks altogether or get bogged down in less important ones.

Strategies to Overcome These Obstacles

1. **Break tasks down**: Large, daunting tasks are prime candidates for procrastination. Break them into smaller, manageable steps. Instead of "Write report," try "Outline report" or "Write introduction."
2. **Use the "two-minute rule"**: If a task will take less than two minutes, do it immediately. This

prevents small tasks from piling up and becoming overwhelming.
3. **Set realistic standards**: Perfection is often the enemy of good. Determine what "good enough" looks like for each task and aim for that.
4. **Practice self-compassion**: Be kind to yourself. Recognize that everyone struggles with these issues sometimes. Beating yourself up only makes it harder to move forward.
5. **Use the "worse draft" technique**: Instead of aiming for perfection, challenge yourself to write the worst possible draft or create the worst possible version of your project. This takes the pressure off and often leads to surprisingly good results.
6. **Visualize success**: Spend a few minutes imagining how good it will feel to complete the task. This can provide motivation to get started.

Remember, done is better than perfect. And starting is often the hardest part. Once you begin, you'll often find the task wasn't as bad as you feared.

The Urgency Trap

The urgency trap is one of the most insidious enemies of effective prioritization. It's the tendency to focus on urgent tasks at the expense of important ones.

Differentiating Between Urgent and Important Tasks

Urgent tasks demand immediate attention. They shout "Now!" They put us in a reactive mode, scrambling to put out fires.

Important tasks contribute to our long-term mission, values, and goals. They're often quieter, less demanding of our immediate attention. But they're the tasks that, when done consistently, lead to significant results.

The problem arises when we consistently prioritize urgent tasks over important ones. We end up spending our days responding to other people's priorities instead of focusing on our own goals.

I fell into this trap early in my career. I was always responsive, always available. I prided myself on my quick email replies and ability to handle last-minute requests. But at the end of each week, I realized I hadn't made progress on my own most important projects.

How to Avoid Getting Caught in the Urgency Trap

1. **Use the Eisenhower Matrix**: This tool, which we'll explore in depth in the next chapter, helps you categorize tasks based on their urgency and importance.
2. **Plan proactively**: Set aside time each week to plan. Identify your most important tasks and schedule them first.
3. **Learn to say no**: Not every urgent request deserves your immediate attention. Practice politely declining or deferring requests that don't align with your priorities.
4. **Create buffers**: Don't schedule every minute of your day. Leave buffer time for unexpected urgent tasks so they don't derail your important work.
5. **Reevaluate regularly**: What seems urgent in the moment may not be important in the long run. Before jumping on an urgent task, take a moment to consider its true importance.

6. **Focus on prevention**: Many urgent tasks arise from lack of planning or neglecting important tasks. By consistently addressing important tasks, you can reduce the number of urgent issues that crop up.

By avoiding these common pitfalls – the myth of multitasking, the traps of procrastination and perfectionism, and the lure of urgency – you'll be well on your way to mastering the art of prioritization.

In the next chapter, we'll explore some proven prioritization frameworks that can help you put these principles into practice. But remember, awareness is the first step. Start paying attention to how these pitfalls show up in your own life. With practice and patience, you can overcome them and become a prioritization pro.

Chapter 3: Proven Prioritization Frameworks

Now that we've identified the common pitfalls of prioritization, let's dive into some practical tools you can use to prioritize effectively. In this chapter, we'll explore four powerful prioritization frameworks: the Eisenhower Matrix, the ABCDE Method, the 80/20 Rule (also known as the Pareto Principle), and the MoSCoW Method.

Each of these frameworks offers a unique approach to prioritization, and you may find that different methods work better for different aspects of your life. The key is to experiment and find what works best for you.

The Eisenhower Matrix

Named after President Dwight D. Eisenhower, who was known for his exceptional ability to organize his workload and productivity, this matrix is a simple but powerful tool for prioritizing tasks based on their urgency and importance.

Quadrants of Urgency and Importance

The Eisenhower Matrix divides tasks into four quadrants:

1. **Urgent and Important** (Do First): These are critical tasks that need to be done immediately. Examples might include crisis management, pressing deadlines, or time-sensitive opportunities.
2. **Important, Not Urgent** (Schedule): These tasks contribute to your long-term goals and should be scheduled. They include things like strategic planning, relationship building, and personal development.
3. **Urgent, Not Important** (Delegate): These tasks are pressing but don't contribute significantly to your goals. They might include certain meetings, some emails, or interruptions. If possible, these should be delegated.
4. **Not Urgent, Not Important** (Eliminate): These tasks don't contribute to your goals and aren't time-sensitive. They're often distractions and should be eliminated where possible.

Practical Examples and Applications

Let's say you're a marketing manager. Here's how you might categorize your tasks:

1. **Urgent and Important**: Responding to a PR crisis, finalizing a presentation for a client meeting tomorrow.
2. **Important, Not Urgent**: Developing next quarter's marketing strategy, researching new marketing trends, team building activities.
3. **Urgent, Not Important**: Answering routine emails, attending a non-essential meeting.
4. **Not Urgent, Not Important**: Scrolling through social media, organizing your desk drawer.

By categorizing your tasks this way, you can clearly see where you should be focusing your energy. The goal is to spend most of your time in Quadrant 2 (Important, Not Urgent), as this is where long-term success and growth happen.

I started using the Eisenhower Matrix when I found myself constantly putting out fires and never making progress on my big goals. It was a wake-up call to see how much time I was spending on urgent but unimportant tasks. By consciously shifting my focus to Quadrant 2 activities, I was able to make significant strides in my long-term projects while reducing stress.

The ABCDE Method

This method, popularized by productivity expert Brian Tracy, involves categorizing tasks based on their relative importance.

Categorizing Tasks by Importance

Here's how it works:

- **A Tasks**: Very important, must do. These have serious consequences if not completed.
- **B Tasks**: Important, should do. These have mild consequences if not completed.
- **C Tasks**: Nice to do, but not essential.
- **D Tasks**: Can be delegated.
- **E Tasks**: Can be eliminated.

How to Apply This Method in Daily Planning

1. Start by listing all your tasks for the day.
2. Go through the list and assign each task a letter from A to E.
3. If you have multiple A tasks, prioritize them further by numbering them A1, A2, A3, etc.
4. Work through your tasks in order, starting with A1.

The key is to resist the temptation to do easier, less important tasks first. Always tackle your A tasks before moving on to B tasks, even if the B tasks are quicker or more enjoyable.

I found this method particularly useful when I was juggling multiple projects with competing deadlines. It forced me to be honest about what was truly important and helped me focus on high-impact activities.

The 80/20 Rule (Pareto Principle)

The Pareto Principle, named after economist Vilfredo Pareto, states that roughly 80% of effects come from 20% of causes. In the context of prioritization, this suggests that 80% of your results come from 20% of your efforts.

Focusing on the Vital Few Tasks That Yield the Most Results

The key to applying the 80/20 rule is to identify which activities fall into that crucial 20%. These are your high-leverage activities – the tasks that give you the biggest bang for your buck.

For example:

- In sales, 20% of your clients might generate 80% of your revenue.
- In project management, 20% of the work (like planning and reviewing) might drive 80% of the project's success.
- In personal productivity, 20% of your daily tasks might contribute to 80% of your progress towards your goals.

Case Studies of the 80/20 Rule in Action

I once consulted for a software company that was struggling with customer support. They were spending equal time on all customer inquiries, leading to backlogs and frustrated high-value clients. By applying the 80/20 rule, they identified that 20% of their customers were responsible for 80% of their revenue. They created a priority support system for these clients, leading to higher satisfaction among key customers and more efficient use of support resources.

In my own work, I realized that 20% of my content creation efforts (usually the initial outlining and key point identification) led to 80% of the value in my final product. By focusing more energy on this crucial

20%, I was able to significantly improve the quality of my work without increasing the total time spent.

MoSCoW Method

The MoSCoW method is particularly useful for project management and personal task prioritization. It categorizes tasks into four groups:

- **Must-have**: Critical for success
- **Should-have**: Important but not necessary for launch
- **Could-have**: Desirable but not necessary
- **Won't-have**: Least-critical, lowest-payoff items or not appropriate at this time

Use Cases for Project Management and Personal Tasks

In project management, the MoSCoW method helps teams agree on priorities and manage stakeholder expectations. For personal tasks, it can help you focus on what's truly essential when you're feeling overwhelmed.

For example, if you're planning a wedding:

- **Must-have**: Venue, officiant, marriage license

- **Should-have**: Photographer, flowers, music
- **Could-have**: Photo booth, fancy invitations, party favors
- **Won't-have**: Fireworks display, celebrity performer

I've found the MoSCoW method particularly helpful when working with clients who have a tendency to treat everything as high priority. It provides a framework for having productive conversations about what's truly essential versus what's just nice to have.

Each of these frameworks offers a different lens through which to view your tasks and priorities. The Eisenhower Matrix helps you balance urgency and importance. The ABCDE Method forces you to make tough choices about relative importance. The 80/20 Rule reminds you to focus on high-leverage activities. And the MoSCoW Method helps you clearly define what's necessary versus what's optional.

As you experiment with these frameworks, you'll likely find that different methods work better in different situations. You might use the Eisenhower Matrix for your weekly planning, the ABCDE Method for daily task management, the 80/20 Rule for strategic decision making, and the MoSCoW Method for project planning.

The key is to start using these tools consistently. In the next chapter, we'll discuss how to personalize these strategies to create a prioritization system that works for you. Remember, the best prioritization system is the one you'll actually use consistently. So let's move on to making these frameworks work for your unique situation and goals.

Chapter 4: Personalizing Your Prioritization Strategy

Now that we've explored several proven prioritization frameworks, it's time to tailor these strategies to your unique needs and circumstances. After all, prioritization isn't one-size-fits-all. What works for a CEO might not work for a freelance artist, and what's effective in your professional life might not be the best fit for your personal tasks.

In this chapter, we'll walk through the process of creating a personalized prioritization strategy. We'll start by assessing your current habits, then move on to aligning your prioritization with your goals, and finally, we'll discuss how to build a flexible system that can evolve with your changing needs.

Assessing Your Current Prioritization Habits

Before we can improve your prioritization skills, we need to understand where you're starting from. This self-assessment will help you identify your strengths and weaknesses when it comes to prioritization.

Exercises for Self-Reflection

1. **The Time Audit**: For one week, keep a detailed log of how you spend your time. Be honest – include everything from work tasks to social media scrolling. At the end of the week, categorize your activities and calculate how much time you spent on each category.
2. **The Energy Map**: Throughout your next workday, rate your energy levels every hour on a scale of 1-10. Note what tasks you were doing during your high-energy and low-energy periods.
3. **The Procrastination Log**: For the next few days, whenever you find yourself procrastinating, write down what task you're avoiding and why you think you're avoiding it.
4. **The Interruption Tracker**: Keep a tally of how often you're interrupted during your workday. Note the source of the interruption (email, colleague, phone, etc.) and whether it was truly urgent.
5. **The Completion Rate**: At the start of each day for a week, write down your top three priorities. At the end of the day, note which ones you completed. Calculate your completion rate at the end of the week.

When I first did these exercises, I was shocked to discover how much time I was wasting on low-value activities. I thought I was being productive by quickly responding to every email, but my time audit showed that I was spending over two hours a day on email alone – time that could have been better spent on strategic tasks.

Identifying Strengths and Weaknesses

After completing these exercises, take some time to reflect on what you've learned. Ask yourself:

- When am I most productive? Least productive?
- What types of tasks do I tend to procrastinate on?
- How often am I working on truly important tasks versus urgent but unimportant ones?
- What are my biggest time-wasters?
- How well do I estimate how long tasks will take?
- Do I tend to overcommit or undercommit?

Be honest with yourself. Remember, the goal isn't to judge, but to understand. We all have strengths and weaknesses when it comes to prioritization. The key is to recognize them so we can build on our strengths and improve our weak areas.

Aligning Prioritization with Goals

Effective prioritization isn't just about getting more done – it's about getting the right things done. To do this, we need to align our daily priorities with our longer-term goals.

Setting SMART Goals

You've probably heard of SMART goals before, but they're worth revisiting in the context of prioritization. SMART stands for:

- **Specific**: Clearly defined and unambiguous
- **Measurable**: Include specific criteria for measuring progress
- **Achievable**: Realistic and attainable
- **Relevant**: Aligns with your broader objectives
- **Time-bound**: Has a defined timeline or deadline

For example, instead of "Improve my coding skills," a SMART goal would be "Complete an advanced Python course and build a web application using Django within the next 3 months."

How to Ensure Your Prioritization Supports Your Long-Term Objectives

1. **Create a goal hierarchy**: Start with your long-term goals (5-10 years), then break them down into medium-term (1-5 years) and short-term (next 12 months) goals. This helps you see how your daily tasks connect to your big-picture aspirations.
2. **Use the "Big Rocks" metaphor**: Imagine your available time is a jar. Your most important goals and responsibilities are big rocks. Less important tasks are pebbles and sand. If you fill your jar with pebbles and sand first, you won't have room for the big rocks. But if you put the big rocks in first, the pebbles and sand can fill in around them.
3. **Do a weekly goal review**: At the start of each week, review your goals and identify the key tasks that will move you closer to achieving them. These become your priorities for the week.
4. **Use the "Three Most Important Tasks" technique**: Each morning, identify the three tasks that, if completed, would make the day a

success in terms of moving you towards your goals. Focus on these before anything else.

5. **Regularly reassess**: Goals can change over time. Schedule quarterly check-ins to ensure your goals still align with your values and aspirations.

I started implementing these strategies when I realized I was busy all the time but not making progress on my big goals. By clearly defining my long-term objectives and aligning my daily priorities with them, I was able to make significant strides in my career and personal projects.

Building a Flexible Prioritization System

Life is unpredictable, and your prioritization system needs to be flexible enough to adapt to changing circumstances while still keeping you focused on what's most important.

Adapting to Changing Circumstances

1. **Use time-blocking, but be prepared to adjust**: Schedule your priorities into your calendar, but leave some buffer time for unexpected tasks or emergencies.

2. **Implement a regular review process**: At the end of each day, week, and month, review what worked and what didn't in your prioritization efforts. Be willing to adjust your approach based on these insights.
3. **Develop decision-making criteria**: Create a set of questions to ask yourself when new opportunities or tasks arise. For example: "Does this align with my goals?" "What would I have to give up to do this?" "What are the long-term implications of saying yes or no?"
4. **Practice the art of re-prioritization**: When unexpected high-priority tasks arise, don't just add them to your to-do list. Take a moment to re-evaluate all your tasks and adjust your priorities accordingly.
5. **Use technology wisely**: There are many apps and tools designed to help with prioritization. Experiment with different ones to find what works for you, but remember – the tool should serve your system, not become the system itself.

Creating a System That Evolves with Your Needs

Your prioritization needs will change as your life and career evolve. Here are some strategies to ensure your system grows with you:

1. **Regular system audits**: Every few months, take a step back and evaluate your entire prioritization system. Is it still serving you well? Are there new challenges it's not addressing?
2. **Seek continuous learning**: Stay open to new prioritization techniques and tools. What works for you now might not be the best approach in a year or two.
3. **Adjust for life changes**: Major life events – a new job, a move, starting a family – can significantly impact your priorities. Be prepared to overhaul your system when these changes occur.
4. **Balance structure and flexibility**: Your system should provide enough structure to keep you focused, but enough flexibility to adapt to changing circumstances. Finding this balance is key to long-term success.
5. **Involve others**: If you have a team or family, involve them in your prioritization process. Their input can provide valuable perspective

and help ensure your priorities align with collective goals.

Remember, the goal is to create a prioritization system that works for you, not against you. It should reduce your stress, not add to it. If you find your system is causing more anxiety than it's alleviating, that's a sign it's time to reassess and adjust.

Personalizing your prioritization strategy is an ongoing process. It requires self-awareness, regular reflection, and a willingness to adapt. But the payoff — a life where you consistently focus on what's truly important to you — is well worth the effort.

In the next chapter, we'll explore how to apply these personalized prioritization strategies in the workplace, where you often have to balance your own priorities with those of your team and organization. But for now, take some time to reflect on what you have learned so far.

Chapter 5: Prioritization in the Workplace

In our work environment of today, mastering the art of prioritization is crucial for success. This chapter explores how to effectively prioritize tasks and manage time in a professional setting, ensuring you achieve your goals without burning out.

Prioritizing in a Team Environment

Working in a team adds an extra layer of complexity to prioritization. You're not just managing your own tasks, but also considering how your work impacts others and fits into the larger organizational goals.

Balancing individual and team priorities

Finding the sweet spot between personal and team objectives is key to thriving in a collaborative workspace. Start by clearly understanding your role and responsibilities within the team. This forms the foundation for aligning your individual priorities with those of your colleagues.

1. **Regularly communicate with your team**: Set up weekly check-ins to discuss ongoing projects and upcoming deadlines. This helps everyone

stay on the same page and adjust priorities as needed.
2. **Use a shared task management system**: Tools like [Trello](#) or [Asana](#) can help visualize team priorities and individual responsibilities.
3. **Be flexible**: Sometimes, you'll need to shift your personal priorities to support a critical team objective. Embrace this flexibility as part of being a valuable team player.
4. **Identify dependencies**: Recognize which of your tasks directly impact your teammates' work. Prioritize these to keep the team's workflow smooth.
5. **Seek clarification**: If you're unsure about the priority level of a task, don't hesitate to ask your manager or team lead for guidance.

Communicating priorities effectively with colleagues

Clear communication is the backbone of successful team prioritization. Here's how to ensure your priorities are understood and respected by your colleagues:

1. **Be transparent**: Share your to-do list and deadlines with your team. This openness helps others understand your workload and capacity.
2. **Use clear language**: When discussing priorities, avoid vague terms. Instead of saying "I'll get to it soon," provide specific timeframes: "I can start on this by Thursday afternoon."
3. **Explain the 'why'**: When you need to focus on a particular task, briefly explain its importance to your role or the team's goals. This context helps others understand and support your priorities.
4. **Learn to say 'no' professionally**: If a new request doesn't align with your current priorities, politely decline or negotiate a later deadline. Explain your current commitments and suggest alternative solutions if possible.
5. **Update regularly**: As priorities shift, keep your team informed. A quick email or message can prevent misunderstandings and keep everyone aligned.

Managing Competing Priorities

In any workplace, you'll often face situations where multiple tasks or projects seem equally urgent.

Learning to navigate these competing priorities is essential for maintaining productivity and reducing stress.

Strategies for negotiation and compromise

When faced with conflicting demands, use these strategies to find a balanced solution:

1. **Assess urgency vs. importance**: Differentiate between tasks that are truly urgent and those that are important but can wait. Use the [Eisenhower Matrix](#) to categorize your tasks.
2. **Identify shared goals**: Look for common objectives between competing priorities. This can help you find solutions that address multiple needs simultaneously.
3. **Propose alternatives**: If you can't meet all demands, suggest creative alternatives. Can deadlines be staggered? Can tasks be divided among team members?
4. **Seek win-win solutions**: Aim for outcomes where all parties feel their needs are at least partially met. This fosters goodwill and cooperation.
5. **Document agreements**: After negotiating priorities, summarize the decisions in writing.

This prevents future misunderstandings and provides a reference point.

Handling conflicting demands from managers and stakeholders

Navigating conflicting requests from higher-ups requires tact and strategy:

1. **Gather all information**: Before responding to conflicting demands, ensure you have a complete understanding of each request's scope and deadline.
2. **Communicate the conflict**: Respectfully inform all parties involved about the competing priorities. They may not be aware of the conflict.
3. **Present a proposed solution**: Come prepared with a suggested plan that attempts to meet the most critical aspects of each request.
4. **Escalate when necessary**: If you can't resolve the conflict, don't hesitate to ask your direct manager or a higher-level decision-maker for guidance.
5. **Stay neutral**: Avoid taking sides or showing favoritism. Focus on finding the best solution for the organization as a whole.

Tools and Techniques for Workplace Prioritization

Leveraging the right tools can significantly enhance your ability to prioritize effectively in the workplace.

Using project management tools

Project management software can transform how you handle priorities:

1. <u>Trello</u>: Great for visual thinkers, Trello uses boards, lists, and cards to help you organize tasks and priorities.
2. <u>Asana</u>: Offers a variety of views (list, board, calendar, timeline) to manage tasks and track progress.
3. <u>Monday.com</u>: Provides customizable workflows and automations to streamline prioritization.
4. <u>Jira</u>: Ideal for software development teams, but adaptable for various project types.
5. <u>Notion</u>: Combines note-taking, databases, and project management for a versatile prioritization tool.

When choosing a tool, consider your team's size, project complexity, and preferred working style. Many tools offer free trials, so experiment to find the best fit.

Time-blocking and calendar management

Effective use of your calendar is a powerful prioritization technique:

1. **Time-blocking**: Allocate specific time slots for different types of tasks. For example, designate 9-11 AM for focused work on high-priority projects.
2. **Color-coding**: Use different colors in your calendar for various types of activities (e.g., blue for meetings, green for deep work, yellow for administrative tasks).
3. **Buffer time**: Schedule short breaks between tasks to allow for unexpected issues or overruns.
4. **Recurring tasks**: Set up recurring events for regular activities like weekly reports or team check-ins.
5. **Review and adjust**: At the end of each week, review your calendar usage and adjust your time-blocking strategy as needed.

By implementing these tools and techniques, you'll be better equipped to manage your priorities in the workplace, leading to increased productivity and reduced stress. So, now that we are done with Prioritization in the Workplace, let's move to how to incorporate Prioritization into your personal life in the next chapter.

Chapter 6: Prioritization Techniques for Personal Life

Mastering prioritization in your personal life is just as crucial as in your professional sphere. This chapter explores strategies to balance various aspects of your life, ensuring you're not just productive, but also fulfilled and healthy.

Balancing Work and Personal Life

In today's always-connected world, the line between work and personal life often blurs. Setting clear boundaries is essential for maintaining a healthy balance and preventing burnout.

The importance of setting boundaries

Establishing and maintaining boundaries between work and personal life is crucial for long-term well-being and productivity. Here's why it matters:

1. **Mental health**: Clear boundaries reduce stress and prevent work-related anxiety from seeping into your personal time.

2. **Relationship quality**: When you're fully present in your personal life, you can build stronger connections with family and friends.
3. **Improved focus**: By compartmentalizing work and personal time, you can give full attention to each when appropriate.
4. **Creativity boost**: Time away from work allows your mind to recharge, often leading to fresh ideas and perspectives.
5. **Long-term sustainability**: Without boundaries, you risk burnout, which can severely impact both your personal and professional life.

Strategies for time management outside of work

Effectively managing your personal time is key to a balanced life. Try these techniques:

1. **Create a personal routine**: Establish a consistent schedule for waking up, exercising, and other daily activities.
2. **Use the [2-minute rule]**: If a task takes less than two minutes, do it immediately instead of putting it off.

3. **Batch similar tasks**: Group errands or household chores to complete them more efficiently.
4. **Learn to say no**: Be selective about commitments. It's okay to decline invitations or requests that don't align with your priorities.
5. **Schedule downtime**: Actively plan for relaxation and hobbies. Treat this time as important as any work commitment.

Prioritizing Health and Well-being

Your health should always be a top priority. It's the foundation that supports all other aspects of your life.

How to make self-care a priority

Self-care isn't selfish; it's necessary. Here's how to ensure you're taking care of yourself:

1. **Schedule it**: Block out time in your calendar for exercise, meditation, or other self-care activities.
2. **Start small**: Begin with achievable goals, like a 10-minute daily walk, and gradually increase.

3. **Create a self-care toolkit:** Identify activities that help you relax and recharge, and keep necessary items easily accessible.
4. **Set reminders:** Use your phone or other devices to remind you to take breaks, drink water, or practice mindfulness.
5. **Learn to recognize burnout signs:** Be aware of physical and emotional signs that you're pushing too hard, and take action early.

The link between well-being and productivity

Understanding how your well-being impacts your productivity can motivate you to prioritize self-care:

1. **Energy management:** Good health habits lead to more consistent energy levels throughout the day.
2. **Improved focus:** Regular exercise and adequate sleep enhance cognitive function and concentration.
3. **Stress resilience:** A well-maintained physical and mental state helps you better handle work pressures.

4. **Creativity boost**: Taking care of your well-being often leads to increased creativity and problem-solving abilities.
5. **Long-term sustainability**: Prioritizing health now can prevent burnout and health issues that could derail your productivity later.

Managing Household and Family Priorities

Balancing personal tasks with family responsibilities requires its own set of prioritization skills.

Techniques for shared prioritization with family members

Effective family prioritization involves everyone:

1. **Family meetings**: Hold regular discussions to align on priorities and distribute tasks.
2. **Shared calendar**: Use a digital calendar that all family members can access and update.
3. **Task rotation**: Assign household chores on a rotating basis to ensure fairness and teach responsibility.
4. **Involve children in planning**: Age-appropriate involvement in

decision-making can teach kids valuable prioritization skills.
5. **Flexibility**: Be prepared to adjust plans when unexpected family needs arise.

Prioritization in parenting and home management

Parenting and managing a home require constant prioritization:

1. **Identify non-negotiables**: Determine the most critical aspects of your parenting and household management that can't be compromised.
2. **Embrace 'good enough'**: Perfectionism can be the enemy of effective prioritization. Sometimes, done is better than perfect.
3. **Teach independence**: Gradually allow children to take on age-appropriate tasks, freeing up your time for other priorities.
4. **Use technology wisely**: Apps for meal planning, grocery shopping, and chore tracking can streamline household management.
5. **Regular decluttering**: Periodically reassess possessions and commitments, letting go of what no longer serves your family's priorities.

By applying these prioritization techniques to your personal life, you can create a more balanced, fulfilling lifestyle that supports both your individual needs and those of your family. We will discuss Prioritization in the Digital Age in the next chapter.

Chapter 7: Prioritization in the Digital Age

We all know the world we live in today is digitally connected, so effective prioritization requires managing not just your physical tasks but also your digital life. This chapter explores strategies for maintaining focus and productivity in an era of constant digital distractions.

Managing Digital Overload

The constant stream of notifications, emails, and social media updates can quickly overwhelm your ability to focus on what's truly important. Learning to manage this digital deluge is crucial for effective prioritization.

Strategies for minimizing digital distractions

1. **Turn off non-essential notifications**: Only allow notifications for truly urgent matters. Everything else can wait until you choose to check it.
2. **Use 'Do Not Disturb' mode**: Most devices have this feature. Use it during focused work periods or personal time.

3. **Create tech-free zones**: Designate certain areas of your home or office as no-phone zones to encourage undistracted focus or relaxation.
4. **Practice digital detox**: Regularly schedule periods where you completely disconnect from digital devices.
5. **Implement the '20-20-20 rule': Every 20 minutes, look at something 20 feet away for 20 seconds. This reduces eye strain and provides mini-breaks from screen time.

Tools for managing emails, notifications, and social media

Several tools can help you regain control over your digital life:

1. Boomerang: This email management tool allows you to schedule emails and set reminders for follow-ups.
2. Freedom: Blocks distracting websites and apps across all your devices.
3. RescueTime: Tracks how you spend your time on digital devices, providing insights to help you optimize your habits.

4. <u>Todoist</u>: A task management app that integrates with email, allowing you to turn messages into actionable items.
5. <u>Forest</u>: A fun app that gamifies staying focused by growing virtual trees when you avoid using your phone.

Prioritization with Digital Tools

While technology can be a source of distraction, it can also be a powerful ally in prioritization when used wisely.

Apps and software that assist with prioritization

1. <u>Evernote</u>: Great for note-taking and organizing ideas across devices.
2. <u>Trello</u>: Visual task management that's excellent for personal and professional use.
3. <u>Any.do</u>: Combines to-do lists, calendars, and reminders in one sleek app.
4. <u>Focus@Will</u>: Provides scientifically designed music to boost concentration and productivity.
5. <u>Notion</u>: A versatile tool for note-taking, project management, and personal knowledge management.

Pros and cons of digital versus analog prioritization methods

Digital methods:

- Pros: Accessible anywhere, easy to update, can set reminders
- Cons: Potential for distraction, reliance on battery life/internet

Analog methods (e.g., paper planner):

- Pros: No distractions, tactile experience, no tech issues
- Cons: Can't set reminders, not always with you, can't easily share

Choose the method that aligns best with your work style and lifestyle. Many people find a combination of both works well.

The Role of Automation in Prioritization

Automation can be a game-changer in prioritization, freeing up your time and mental energy for high-value tasks.

How to use automation to reduce workload and focus on important tasks

1. **Email filters**: Set up rules to automatically sort incoming emails into appropriate folders.
2. <u>IFTTT</u> **(If This Then That)**: Create custom automations between various apps and services.
3. <u>Zapier</u>: Similar to IFTTT, but with more advanced features for complex workflows.
4. **Smart home devices**: Use voice commands to set reminders, add to shopping lists, or control your environment.
5. <u>TextExpander</u>: Create shortcuts for frequently used text snippets to save time on repetitive typing.

Examples of automation tools and their uses

1. <u>Buffer</u>: Schedule social media posts in advance, freeing up daily time.
2. <u>LastPass</u>: Automate password management for quick, secure logins.
3. <u>Calendly</u>: Automate scheduling by letting others book time slots based on your availability.
4. <u>YNAB</u> **(You Need A Budget)**: Automate aspects of personal finance management.
5. <u>Hootsuite</u>: Manage and schedule content across multiple social media platforms.

By leveraging these digital strategies and tools, you can create a more streamlined, focused approach to prioritization in the digital age. Remember, the goal is to make technology work for you, not the other way around. So, take your time and reminisce on what you have learned in this chapter. After which We will be looking at Developing Long-Term Prioritization Habit in the next chapter.

Chapter 8: Developing Long-Term Prioritization Habits

Mastering prioritization isn't a one-time achievement; it's an ongoing process that requires consistent effort and refinement. This chapter focuses on how to build and maintain effective prioritization habits that will serve you well into the future.

Creating Sustainable Habits

The key to long-term success in prioritization lies in developing habits that you can maintain consistently over time.

The importance of consistency and discipline

Consistency is the bedrock of habit formation. Here's why it matters:

1. **Neuroplasticity**: Regular practice rewires your brain, making prioritization skills more automatic over time.
2. **Compound effect**: Small, consistent actions lead to significant improvements over the long term.

3. **Reduced decision fatigue:** When prioritization becomes habitual, you expend less mental energy on daily decisions.
4. **Increased confidence:** Consistently meeting your priorities builds self-trust and confidence in your abilities.
5. **Improved productivity:** As prioritization becomes second nature, you'll accomplish more with less stress.

Techniques for building and maintaining prioritization habits

1. **Start small:** Begin with one or two prioritization techniques and gradually add more as you become comfortable.
2. **Use the 'habit stacking' method:** Attach new prioritization habits to existing routines. For example, review your priorities right after your morning coffee.
3. **Create a supportive environment:** Set up your workspace to encourage good prioritization habits. Keep your planning tools easily accessible.

4. **Track your progress**: Use a habit tracker app or journal to monitor your consistency. Seeing your progress can be motivating.
5. **Celebrate small wins**: Acknowledge your successes, no matter how small. This positive reinforcement helps cement new habits.

Periodic Review and Adjustment

Regular review of your prioritization strategies is crucial for long-term success. It allows you to adapt to changing circumstances and continuously improve your approach.

The role of regular reviews in effective prioritization

Periodic reviews serve several important functions:

1. **Reality check**: They help you assess whether your current priorities align with your long-term goals.
2. **Identify patterns**: Regular reviews can reveal recurring issues or successes in your prioritization approach.

3. **Course correction**: They provide opportunities to adjust your strategies before small issues become big problems.
4. **Learning opportunity**: Each review is a chance to reflect on what worked well and what didn't, enhancing your prioritization skills over time.
5. **Motivation boost**: Seeing progress can reinvigorate your commitment to effective prioritization.

How to adjust your priorities as life circumstances change

Life is dynamic, and your prioritization strategies should be too. Here's how to adapt:

1. **Schedule regular check-ins**: Set aside time monthly or quarterly to review your priorities and methods.
2. **Be honest with yourself**: Assess whether your current priorities truly reflect what's most important to you now.
3. **Stay flexible**: Be willing to let go of priorities that no longer serve you, even if they once seemed important.

4. **Seek feedback**: Ask trusted friends, family, or colleagues for their perspective on your priorities and balance.
5. **Experiment with new methods**: Don't be afraid to try new prioritization techniques if your current ones aren't working as well as they used to.

Overcoming Setbacks and Staying on Track

Even with the best intentions, you'll likely face challenges in maintaining your prioritization habits. Learning to navigate these setbacks is crucial for long-term success.

Strategies for dealing with disruptions and setbacks

1. **Practice self-compassion**: Don't beat yourself up over temporary lapses. Treat setbacks as learning opportunities.
2. **Identify triggers**: Pay attention to what causes you to fall off track. Understanding these triggers can help you prevent future setbacks.
3. **Have a backup plan**: Develop contingency strategies for common disruptions to your routine.

4. **Start fresh**: If you've had a bad day or week, don't wait for a "perfect" time to restart. Begin again immediately.
5. **Learn from each setback**: After each disruption, reflect on what happened and how you can handle similar situations better in the future.

How to regain focus after a lapse in prioritization

1. **Mini reset**: Take a few minutes to breathe deeply and mentally reset your focus.
2. **Review your goals**: Remind yourself of your big-picture objectives to reignite your motivation.
3. **Start with a small win**: Choose one easy task to complete, building momentum to tackle larger priorities.
4. ****Use the 'Pomodoro Technique'**: Break your work into 25-minute focused sessions with short breaks in between.
5. **Eliminate immediate distractions**: Clear your workspace, turn off notifications, and create an environment conducive to focus.

By developing sustainable habits, regularly reviewing and adjusting your approach, and learning to overcome setbacks, you'll build a strong foundation for long-term success in prioritization. Remember, it's not about perfection, but consistent progress over time.

My Final Word: The Path to a Balanced and Productive Life

As we wrap up our exploration of prioritization, it's clear that mastering this skill is not just about getting more done—it's about creating a life that aligns with your values and goals. Let's recap the key principles we've covered and look at how you can continue to refine your prioritization skills moving forward.

Recap of Key Principles

Throughout this book, we've covered several crucial aspects of effective prioritization:

1. **Workplace prioritization**: We explored how to balance individual and team priorities, manage competing demands, and leverage tools for better time management.
2. **Personal life prioritization**: We discussed strategies for maintaining work-life balance, prioritizing health and well-being, and managing family responsibilities.
3. **Digital age challenges**: We looked at ways to manage digital overload, use technology to our

advantage, and harness the power of automation.
4. **Long-term habit formation**: We emphasized the importance of consistency, regular review, and adapting to life's changes.

These principles form the foundation of a comprehensive approach to prioritization that can transform both your professional and personal life.

The Ongoing Journey of Prioritization

It's important to recognize that prioritization is not a destination, but a continuous journey. As your life evolves, so too will your priorities and the strategies you use to manage them.

Understanding that prioritization is a continuous process

1. **Embrace change**: Your priorities will shift over time, and that's okay. Regular reassessment keeps your efforts aligned with what truly matters to you.
2. **Keep learning**: Stay open to new prioritization techniques and tools. What works best for you

may change as your responsibilities and goals evolve.
3. **Practice self-awareness**: Continuously monitor how you feel about your current priorities. Are they energizing you or draining you? Adjust accordingly.
4. **Seek balance**: Strive for a harmonious blend of professional achievement, personal fulfillment, and overall well-being.
5. **Be patient with yourself**: Remember that mastering prioritization is a lifelong skill. Celebrate your progress and learn from your missteps.

Encouragement to keep refining and adapting prioritization strategies

1. **Experiment regularly**: Try new prioritization methods or tools every few months to see if they enhance your productivity.
2. **Share and learn from others**: Discuss prioritization strategies with colleagues, friends, or in online communities. You might discover valuable new approaches.

3. **Reflect on your successes**: Take note of which strategies have worked well for you and why. This insight can guide your future choices.
4. **Stay flexible**: Be willing to abandon methods that no longer serve you, even if they worked well in the past.
5. **Set prioritization goals**: Just as you set goals in other areas of life, set specific objectives for improving your prioritization skills.

Final Words of Encouragement

As you continue on your prioritization journey, remember these key points:

1. **Trust the process**: Effective prioritization takes time to master. Trust that your efforts will yield significant benefits over time.
2. **Focus on progress, not perfection**: There will always be room for improvement. Celebrate your growth rather than striving for an unattainable ideal.
3. **Stay true to your values**: Let your core values guide your priorities. This alignment brings a sense of purpose and fulfillment to your efforts.

4. **Be kind to yourself**: On days when prioritization feels challenging, treat yourself with compassion. Tomorrow is always a new opportunity to refocus.
5. **Inspire others**: As you improve your prioritization skills, you may find yourself in a position to help others. Sharing your journey can be rewarding and reinforcing.

The potential impact of effective prioritization on your personal and professional life is profound. By consistently applying the principles and strategies we've discussed, you're setting yourself up for:

- Increased productivity and efficiency
- Reduced stress and overwhelm
- Improved work-life balance
- Greater sense of control over your time and energy
- Enhanced ability to achieve your most important goals

Remember, prioritization is not just about doing more—it's about doing what matters most. As you move forward, carry with you the knowledge that each small decision to prioritize effectively is a step towards a more balanced, fulfilling, and successful life.

Your journey to mastering prioritization starts now. Embrace the process, stay committed to your growth, and watch as your ability to focus on what truly matters transforms your life, one priority at a time.

Appendices

Appendix A: Prioritization Worksheets

To help you put the principles and strategies from this book into practice, here are some printable templates for daily, weekly, and monthly prioritization:

1. **Daily Priority Planner**
- Top 3 priorities for the day
- Time-blocked schedule
- End-of-day reflection
2. **Weekly Goal Setting Worksheet**
- Review of previous week's accomplishments
- Top 5 goals for the coming week
- Potential obstacles and solutions
3. **Monthly Priority Review**
- Reflection on past month's priorities
- Alignment check with long-term goals
- Adjustments for the coming month
4. **Eisenhower Matrix Template**
- Quadrants for urgent/important tasks
- Space for action items in each quadrant
5. **Personal Values Assessment**

- List of core values
- Current priorities alignment check

These worksheets are designed to be simple yet effective tools to support your prioritization journey. Feel free to adapt them to best suit your needs and working style.

Appendix B: Recommended Reading and Resources

To further your understanding and application of prioritization principles, consider exploring these additional resources:

Books

1. "Deep Work" by Cal Newport
2. "Essentialism" by Greg McKeown
3. "The 7 Habits of Highly Effective People" by Stephen Covey
4. "Getting Things Done" by David Allen
5. "Atomic Habits" by James Clear

Tools

1. Trello for visual task management

2. RescueTime for time tracking and productivity insights
3. Todoist for to-do list management
4. Forest for focused work sessions

These resources offer a wealth of additional insights and strategies to support your ongoing prioritization journey.

Appendix C: Glossary of Terms

To ensure clarity and common understanding, here's a glossary of key terms used throughout the book:

1. **Prioritization**: The action or process of deciding the relative importance or urgency of a thing or things.
2. **Time-blocking**: A time management method that divides your day into blocks of time, each dedicated to accomplishing a specific task or group of tasks.
3. **Eisenhower Matrix**: A prioritization tool that categorizes tasks based on their urgency and importance.
4. **Deep work**: Coined by Cal Newport, it refers to professional activities performed in a state of

distraction-free concentration that push your cognitive capabilities to their limit.
5. **Pareto Principle (80/20 rule)**: The idea that roughly 80% of effects come from 20% of causes.
6. **Productivity**: The effectiveness of productive effort, especially in terms of the rate of output per unit of input.
7. **Work-life balance**: The equilibrium between personal life and career work.
8. **Digital detox**: A period during which a person refrains from using electronic devices such as smartphones or computers, regarded as an opportunity to reduce stress or focus on social interaction in the physical world.
9. **Habit stacking**: A technique where you stack a new habit on top of a current habit.
10. **Pomodoro Technique**: A time management method using a timer to break work into intervals, traditionally 25 minutes in length, separated by short breaks.

This glossary serves as a quick reference to help you better understand and apply the concepts discussed in the book.

ABOUT THE AUTHOR

Harrell Howard is a prolific author and thought leader, specializing in a diverse array of subjects that cater to both personal and professional development. With a deep passion for empowering readers through knowledge, Harrell has penned numerous best-selling books, each offering practical insights and actionable strategies across various fields.

Harrell Howard combines a rich background in technology, marketing, and personal development to deliver content that is both insightful and practical.

When he's not writing, Harrell enjoys exploring new tech, market trends, and sharing his knowledge via speaking engagements and workshops. His drive for lifelong learning & passion for helping others is evident in his book.

www.ingramcontent.com/pod-product-compliance
Lightning Source LLC
Chambersburg PA
CBHW070353230526
45471CB00006B/2551